Blessed Arrangement

Poems by Larry Levy

atmosphere press

Copyright © 2021 Larry Levy

Published by Atmosphere Press

Cover photo by Rob Hyner
Cover design by Nick Courtright

No part of this book may be reproduced
except in brief quotations and in reviews
without permission from the publisher.

Blessed Arrangement
2021, Larry Levy

atmospherepress.com

Contents

III. Love May Be Wiser Than Anyone Knows   45

If I am not for myself, who will be for me?

But if I am only for myself, what then am I?

And if not now, when?

Rabbi Hillel

I.

This is Our Street.
        And You're Not Us.

Board Meeting

To hell with polar bears,
their cubs in dugout dens.
To hell with satanic fires.
We are businessmen.

Fuel brewing beneath this frost
we siphon to the top.
Regardless of the cost,
oil's our cash crop,

our communion bread,
our sacramental wine.
Some dolphins may be dead,
but God's elect are fine.

More than fine, we're proud
to resist, to stand alone.
To hell with the science crowd.
We rule our spinning stone.

George from Poland

When they came, herding parents,
brothers, sisters, playmates,
elders, cousins, infants
into a few narrow streets,

we obeyed. Choice was the first
privilege to disappear. Used to edicts,
Papa shared stale bread, an old cursed
image of ourselves. Then they sicced

the dogs on us, huddled in fears
of night trains, the work farms.
Papa reassured: *Has anyone died from stars,
from numbers burned on arms?*

Somehow, I outlasted cholera,
beatings, daily selections. I alone
came to Detroit, America,
removed the tattoo. Moved on.

One morning in a café
I heard voices: *The ovens are a lie.
Anne Frank, six million—baloney,* they say.
Papa's words return: *You must survive.*

*People will not believe.
You must not give in, must try.
Show them. Roll up your sleeve.*

Oh, Father, of what then did we die?

Black Monday

You've kept ledgers to the penny,
prepared agendas, gone for coffee—
how many decades has it been?

Tomorrow you won't be coming in.
Sorry we have to meet like this.
It's my obligation to dismiss

those for whom we have no use.
I could give you some excuse,
But when Upstairs says you're gone

I'm the man who gets it done,
The Corner Office, the advanced degree
in Industrial Psychology.

My training means I am equipped
to walk you through this exit script:
Close your desk, please. Do it now.

Disconnect. I'll show you how
to pack your profession in a box.
Here are the doors and here the locks.

Security will show you out,
escort you to the parking lot.
Personnel will be our witness.

You're upset? Don't be nervous.
As they say, it's merely business.
Thank you for your years of service.

The Holocaust Memorial Quiz

The Museum's computer game
offers scenarios. You decide
to take refuge in the countryside
or burrow beneath your home.

Maybe cross the eastern river,
acquiring another tongue.
Are you safe? For how long?
Will the forest provide cover?

Choose! But any choice
most likely will result
in a catastrophic fault.
So rarely a surprise

beats the odds. If you survive
to play another round,
try the swamp's high ground
or the haymow. You might live.

Surely the milkmaid must,
the woodsman, the priest?
Surely this child at least
will not betray your trust?

What's plain on paper—
so sensible, so safe—
reveals in real life
your neighbor's not your neighbor.

Because

For the children

He cannot see them, though they are there
right in front of him, huddled on the floor
like a litter of pups. Stray socks in a drawer.
Mismatched. Dark faces, dark hair,

eyes barely open, red with grime.
Voices, from crying and not being heard,
silenced to a whisper. A croak from a bird
blown from the nest. Day and night the same,

world without end, endless confinement
without sun, without blue or green
or breeze. And this by decree, by design,
more than callous, more than malignant.

Because he will not see, is more than content
with how things are. Because he is fine.

Packing

This is in this morning's news,
this video clip of a hawk-faced guy
wearing neither shirt nor shoes.
He is firing into the evening sky

to arrest the stranger's attention,
especially this nearby kid, flinching low
as if in Hollywood this posture would
redirect the bullet's blow

to his cranium. Now the barrel
aimed at the heart has nothing to discuss.
End of story, and this is the moral:
This Is Our Street. And You're Not Us.

Hitlerland

> *…at least he believed what he said.*

This is how it happens
if history is correct.
This is how you witness
what you least expect.

While echoing his songs,
perceiving not a hint,
his bragging and his banners
seem insignificant.

Toasting another lager
from Munich to Berlin,
you join in all the shouting,
eager to begin,

eager to target neighbors
who must vacate this place,
to listing those who lack
correct blood in the face.

You say *Give him a chance.*
You will guide him to repent.
His vitriol, his ranting,
isn't really what he meant.

Indelible in the Hippocampus

Clearing throats and tabletop clutter,
eleven gentlemen straighten their ties,
tap their pencils, sip bottled water.

It would help your cause if you do not stutter,
says the Chairman, and meet our eyes.
They perceive before them a wounded daughter.

She gathers memories, sits up straight.
One listener, inhaling, sighs.
One consults a cell that cannot wait.

Are you certain the Accused was there?
Are you certain what you said you meant.
I am certain one hundred percent.

But you were unclear about when and where.
You know how it ended, how it began,
but perhaps it was a different man?

To what degree, then, can you swear
it was him, and without consent?
I am certain one hundred percent.

Did anyone wrestle with his doubts?
The Chair closes debate and counts the votes.
So it is settled, and so they went

each into his handheld phone
noting who approved and what they spent
to claim this victory as their own.

A Kid I Coached

Although enrolled in Christian school,
avoiding movies and most TV,
he joked the Golden Rule
meant *do to others before they do to me.*

He showed this on the soccer field—
doggedly dismantling every foe,
defending bigger boys to yield,
stopping and starting just so,

maneuvering a give and go,
tapping a left footer into the net.
Where others barked, he was slow
to speak, preferring a quiet

smile when complimented
by opponents who knew his name.
To teammates, he represented
confidence. They wished for the same.

So, who is this person, forty years since,
livid about Takers, Voting Cheats,
Women, Blacks, Immigrants—
all those trampling his God-given rights?

In his Facebook photo, still lean,
he sports his childhood Cross.
But why the frown, the angry tone,
the petulant sense of loss?

He dismisses my point-of-view as fake,
forgiving me for old time's sake.
I want to say *You were given a lot.*
I thought I knew you. Realize I do not.

Our Daily News

During recess, we split into two groups,
each on either side of a line in the sand,
daring an opponent, a lightweight or dupe,
to cross into no-man's land.

Today, every day, an adult version
plays out: *Red Rover, Red Rover...*
Many sworn to protect our nation
stand silent. But many cross over.

They smile on the evening news,
laughing even, as their Boss
signs papers dismissing rules.
There is no line he will not cross.

Renushka's Diary

My father's gone, but who knows where?
They took him to shovel snow in the street
then hacked off his beard and most of his hair.
Who is responsible for his fate?

My mother's in Warsaw the last I knew.
Sometimes I receive a note from her.
Notwithstanding, I miss her so
and wonder who can say for sure

if she is well, if she is warm.
Will we embrace one another again?
God, keep us all from want and harm.
Reunite us. But who knows when?

In my diary I embrace my dreams,
my teachers, my friends. I think about love,
my boyfriend, Z. How perfect he seems!
He wants us to stay together, to survive

as a couple, marry after the war.
But who knows when this war will end?
Now they've taken my winter fur.
My diary remains my only friend.

I have no memory of what warm is.
Every day I scribble my rhymes,
am so in love they call me Mrs.
Mama called me by pet names

I haven't heard in many years.
All I know—the heartless regimes
are responsible for my tears.
But who is responsible for my dreams?

Tit for Tat

I would do this for you
if you would do that for me.
You are the people who
I send my people to see.
It's how I often succeed—
if often illegally.

So what? I have what you need,
and you have something, too.
Let's call it a favor, so you'd
be smart to do what I say.
It's business, if often crude.
I do this every day.

And no one else need know
about our quid pro quo.

Vicar of Family Values

Awake at night, sweat running cold,
he dreams of Wilbur petting Mr. Ed,
Lassie licking young Joey's face,

Woody Woodpecker flipping the bird,
Mickey and Minnie minus their pants.
What does he fear? A wide stance

in a rest room stall? Denying The Word?
Co-mingling a diseased race
with the anointed? Lover to wed

lover, to have and to hold?
No! No union between dog and cat!
Certainly he will have none of that!

In the heat of his morning shower,
scrubbing each part the Lord has made—
including both sacred and profane—

he emerges pure of body, his soul pristine,
and girds his loins, steadfast, unafraid,
armed with apocalyptic power,

and gallops off to his next Crusade—
Satan's Diversity Day—where all will cower
before He Who Must Be Obeyed.

Twice Blessed

In his eyes he stands taller than his rivals
although most have achieved some success,
a measure of learning, possessions,
some renown, some power.

In his eyes all are flawed while he is flawless,
and he would have them bend, have them cower
and flinch. So he would appear above nations,
their history and hopes nothing, nor their survival.

In him, no music of the spheres, no poetry or art.
In him, no reason but passions, without compassion
for another's heart, another's struggle from birth.
They are not under the same star nor of the same earth.

But, in time, to the weak and mighty alike,
heaven's waters rush, cleansing in their wake.
Mountains of injustice will vanish where it rained.
In time, neither mercy nor justice are strained.

Toxic Stew

A pinch of this, a smidge of that
is who you are and say I am.
You contribute to the pot
fistfuls of habanero—Bam!

Stir the onions till they sweat,
caramelize, nearly disappear.
Bitterroot, nightshade—don't forget
ghost pepper. Is it clear

this is not a morning meal?
No matter how you dice or chop
or serve it for the commonweal,
no matter how you plate it up,

no biscuit will soak up this sop.
No matter how you try to cram
this gumbo, it's still polecat slop
of what you are and say I am.

His Base

He leads us to believe,
to stand at his right arm.
He pours pain into the hollow
vacuum in our hearts,

makes us feel alive,
keeps us from all harm.
In uniform we follow
his intoxicating sermon,

hating what he hates,
outsiders and the vermin.
His words—but more--his wink—
lead us from dead ends,

lead us not to think.
We heed his glance or nod.
His friends are now our friends,
and he is now our God.

A Rouse of Clerihews

Because Barr lacked a heart, he
bowed to the Grand Old Party.
Was it what they represented
or their brains so well fermented?

McConnell, Mitch,
a son of a bitch,
is also the spawn of a turtle,
his heart and soul infertile.

Lyndsay Graham
doesn't give a damn
to value science or fact
when his Court is so well-packed.

Steve Mnuchin honors Trump
for draining the swamp.
Trump claims Steve is world class.
Especially when he's kissing ass.

Stephen Miller may have a soul
buried in the blackest hole
of his heart. Or not.
If he once felt compassion, he forgot.

Donald Trump
is thick and plump.
Although he insists he's fit,
psychiatrists doubt it.

At the Polling Place

I read the Pledge in English,
en Español as well.
Can name the fifty states,
likewise each capitol.

I can reasonably recite
the Gettysburg Address.
Treasure life and liberty,
the pursuit of happiness.

I know the forty-five
Presidents by rote.
And no one may deprive
me of my precious vote.

II.

Come Live With Me and Be My Love

One Morning in Michigan

for Jack Fogarty

Driving to Clare this morning, I
thought about the goose-gray sky,

the pinpoints on my windshield, and
how much it seemed like Ireland,

where, says Jack, my Irish friend,
it mists Cork to Sligo without end,

from Birr to Belfast, clouding down,
greening pasture, hill, and town.

Says Jack, It's true, but don't forget
your slicker keeps you dry, and yet

there's little cause to fret or frown—
the Irish rain's not really wet.

The Zapotecan

Salomon grew up in a mountain pueblo
many miles from the paved streets of Oaxaca,
one of thirteen born to his mother, Hilario,
who died recently and is buried in el panteón.

Ordinarily on Día de Muertos
he would be with his family to place tamales
and mezcal on her altar, to tell stories and sing songs.
His father, now 93, lives with Salomon in the city,
and if he's up to it they will make the trip back.

Salomon's children have attended university.
One is a lawyer, one an architect.
Salomon had six years of school in the pueblo
and married a girl he has known since childhood.
Was she the only girlfriend you had? I ask.
He smiles: *No, but it was different then.*
Our parents told us who to marry.
Now they have children before they marry.

He hunted for food to help feed the family.
Occasionally he brought home a deer or iguana.
An iguana? What does iguana taste like?
Well, like chicken. He smiles at his own chiste.
The long tail is all meat.

His mother made the best mole, sometimes with iguana.
Now his wife and sisters make the mole—good,
but not quite as good as he remembers his mother's.
I suggest *Perhaps she stirred it with her little finger.*

Today it is forbidden to hunt endangered creatures.
Once there were armadillos—now, not so much.
And even after the government protected them
he confesses he still occasionally hunted iguana.

What is the secret to your father's long life?
Salomon is quiet, thinking.
Perhaps it is the mole amarillo con iguana?
He bursts into laughter. *Yes, perhaps,* he smiles.
That, and mezcal.

In the Oaxacan hills and valley everybody drinks mezcal,
the fiery brew from processed agave plants
which grow wild and on cultivated plantations—
mercados ordering barrels of mezcal,
distributing it all over Mexico and beyond.
Their salespeople deliver sample bottles to bars
and cafes in hopes they will buy by the case.

On the farms, in the pueblos, in some private restaurants
many Oaxaqueños brew their own mezcal,
some of it clear as water, some shades of amber.
They avoid paying taxes on it.

Salomon left the mountains for the city
to make a better life for his children.
He drives a cab, guides touristas like us.
To do this he studied English and learned to drive.
He appears to be doing well with both,
a Zapotec man who no longer remembers his language.

He tells us how to say *hello* in Zapotec,
in our ears an odd combination of sounds
and all but unpronounceable.
But we try. We want to see Salomon smile.

Pura Vida on Wixom Lake

for Sarah and Andy Schulz

Here in this nearly autumn of Michigan
there are few cafes, indoors or out.
None that I'm aware of serve plantain,
gallo pinto, or casado. And I doubt

that the cottonwoods and white pines
harbor monkeys howling at dawn,
or sloths, foot by foot, traversing the vines,
or iguanas sunning on the dock or lawn.

The water is cold, but I swim anyway,
emerging into a towel, your arms.
Such a bright, breathtaking sky
before clouds come, and the storms.

One hummingbird darts back and forth
sipping honeysuckle, lilies, fox glove.
The lake ripples, a breeze from the north,
while we sip whiskey, toasting our love.

More Than Dust

Motoring up highway five,
we came upon a small café.
An ancient lady stirred a pot
in the middle of our day.

She conjured a condiment,
famous in those parts,
the ingredients a secret
of her culinary arts.

Some peaches we supposed?
Mustard and brown sugar?
A hint of cayenne pepper?
A splash of vinegar?

Magical the hostess said,
sprinkled on brown beans,
even better on your fries,
and best on collard greens.

Whatever, it was alive,
each mouthful sweet and hot.
When we happened by years later
we beheld an empty lot,

no restaurant, no handmade sign
marked the hamlet's best.
No baked and barbecued cuisine,
nor the dressing that impressed.

And no local recalled the place,
not the sorceress, not her sauce.
And no one felt the absence
was notable or a loss.

Old Mesilla

Our friend back East offered advice
as we embarked on a cross country drive:
Your destination's a dicey place

where some touristas don't survive,
where you dare not show your face
or venture after dark away from home.

So if we prefer to stay alive
we best bolt doors and stay in bed?
But hasn't it been a century since

a guy caught a bullet from Billy the Kid?
We hear that once upon a time
this valley witnessed many a crime,

robbing a bank, the Pony Express,
knifing the dealer who won a lot.
Back then, la posada meant progress,

clean sheets, a chamber pot.
I don't know this pueblo, I confess.
But this café's a tranquil spot.

Exchange Student

I offer my hand. He offers a fish,
a carp, nearly comatose.

Heavily inflected, leaning close,
he says it is his American wish
to prepare for us a native dish—

a mound of rice with sauce of fire.
Tomorrow he'll concoct the same,
a something many-lettered name,

unpronounceable to our hearing
and undigestible, though endearing.
So, he chops away, stirring the wok,

sopping his plate with papadums.
Then we lie awake, tossing Tums,

driving to the all-night pharmacy,
celebrating international diplomacy.

But if I am only for myself, what then am I?

Why am I thinking of the writer Isaak Babel,
born in the Jewish ghetto of Odessa, who spent
his early years in the Black Sea port Nikolaev?
In 1900, because Jews were forbidden to live
in Moscow, St. Petersburg, Kiev and other localities,
Odessa had more Jews than any city in the Empire.

Between 1881 and 1917 two million Jews left Russia,
mostly for America, but some to anywhere
they could procure papers, legal or often illegal.
They also went to Poland, Germany, France,
England, Palestine, Argentina—most not wealthy,
most speaking no language other than Yiddish.

Why did they leave? To preach Bolshevik dogma?
Spread the Plague? Poison village wells? Perform
ritual murder on gentile boys? Celebrate
the murder of the Christian Messiah? Contribute
to the International Jewish Conspiracy as described
in the Protocols of the Elders of Zion?

Among the many who came was a young couple,
20 and 19, brother and sister according to their papers,
but by their real names really husband and wife.
He was dark, handsome, one of the rare Jews
admitted to Russian university, to study architecture.
He read Spinoza, played mandolin, never saw his parents again.

She was fair, plain until she smiled, her eyes dancing,
a lover of talk, music. She danced at weddings.
Her siblings looked to them for advice in the New World.
He never raised his voice. They raised three children,
two surviving into adulthood. They kept kosher, attended shul.
He worked as a carpenter, a roofer, dug ditches, whatever it took.

They learned English, heavily accented, became citizens.
After World War II, asked by a reporter about refugees,
she replied *You have to help people.* I still have that clipping—
dated 1947, the year I was born—now yellowed, faded,
its message fresh and vivid upon my heart:
 We have to help people.

Ode to the Melanzana

To conjugate *to eggplant*
note its purple present tense,

royal at the bottom, crowned
with spikes in self-defense.

Sometimes white and rounded, hence
its name and odd-sounding others.

Sometimes oval like a bean,
addressed in Europe *aubergine,*

prepped by every nation's mothers—
tomato, potato are its brothers—

grilled, pureed, or chopped and chewy,
or with squash in ratatouille,

parmigiana, spicy bhartha,
baba ghanoush, cold caponata.

With antioxidants—which are good!
By picky eaters misunderstood.

I've tried to marinate and sear it.
My grandchildren won't get near it.

Come Live With Me and Be My Love

On a mountain once, I saw
giant birds, Great Green Macaw
eating mountain almonds raw.

One of the most wondrous things I've seen.
Through the palms—twelve, no, thirteen,
morning blue, Caribbean green.

Strangest was one's chiseled beak
but stranger still an electric shriek
she telegraphed from peak to peak,

an oath to her monogamy:
Come to my mountain almond tree.
She seemed, I swear, to speak to me.

You know, I could not duplicate
any vow to be her mate.
But she was green, and she was great!

Howlers

Always before early light
filters through the canopy,
a disembodied voice, a ghost,
bellows from the tallest tree.

From the hill, from the coast,
it carries as if amplified:
*Sleepers! It is I, the most
scary singer God has made!*

I am Shadow you cannot see.
I am Trembling Leaves above.
Narrow your eye. It may be me
calling. And then I move.

Les Bon Temps

We flew in for the weekend feeling merry.
Walked to the dock to catch the ferry
across to the west bank, a family café,
and I ordered gumbo and you étouffée.

Both dishes so thick, you stuck in a fork
it stood up tall and straight as a stork.
And the parlez around us, jambalaya stew,
conjured gris-gris from the bayou.

After dinner, Mama offered her hand.
Her son on vocals struck up the band—
fiddle, triangle, washboard and thimble.
So I tried to dance who had never been nimble.

C'mon, darlin', said Mama. You just never been taught.
In here ain't nobody says cannot.
She taught me two-step. She taught me twirl
in waltz-time, where you spin the girl.

We joined hands, s'il vous plait,
circling, shuffling, a sly sashay.
Come be with me, cher. Avec moi?
You're my joie de vivre. Et toi?

We danced in Thibodaux, in Lafayette,
from cajun folks learned swamp etiquette.
And it all began in that welcoming joint
across the river on Algiers Point.

Above the Sanford Dam

Verde, que te quiero verde...

My loved ones think it's a mistake
to swim alone in the middle of the lake.
How can you do that—bless my soul!
Aren't you afraid for goodness sake?

I know the dear hearts wish me well
but worry I will drown in Hell.
They fret about cramps, the bellyache,
a log ringing my cranium's bell.

But here the water's quiet, still.
Everywhere it's green, opaque.
I sometimes breaststroke, mostly crawl,
breathing in rhythm, wholly awake.

Por Antonio, Por Su Hospitalidad

We shared your bread, arrachera steak,
cebollas roasted on a wood-fired grill.
While you sang off-key we ate our fill,
laughing, crying, until daybreak.

Now we hear you are not only loud
but certain your dearest friends are fools:
*Of course, the Jewish lying crowd
bathed in Birkenau's in-ground pools.*

*Of course, their numbers are inflated.
Pesticides? Ovens? Por favor—
Weren't they rodents, lice-infected,
Europe's misfortune? It was war.*

You ramble on, tequila-slurred.
Your listeners leave without a word.

Science Teacher

for David Gill

As spring unfolded, he folded up.
Hair uprooted. The rest went gray.
He wilted a bit more each day.
On weekends he sat for his drip.
Was it helping? He wouldn't say.

Each day his clothes hung looser
on his once pear-shaped frame.
Some knew he was chasing time,
so students tried to be nicer,
but many were mostly the same,

preening, making a fuss,
quarrelsome, loud in the hall.
Well, they were in middle school
practicing tribal rites, how to cuss,
to live forever, be forever cool.

Some could not deny his cells'
disruption, the yellowish skin,
pale egg yolk, sulfur, amber resin.
They learned the color of chemicals,
but it did not arrest their attention.

They thought him an odd fellow,
walking them through a scraggly field
naming young weeds. But he was old,
which they would never be, nor yellow,
nor anything but green or gold.

Denial

Workdays it begins before dawn,
the preparation of hot morning joe
with a splash of Irish, more than one
cup, more than one splash. You know,
it's a long day ahead, filled with strife.
So, one for movement, one for life.

Pack the thermos with *little water*,
as Russians call it. To stay awake.
To stay alert. To speak in clever
bon mots for the clients at work.
For lively and worrisome colleagues
alike, my wise and witty tongue.

On Saturdays the menu varies,
not the routine. Light one Marlboro
off the other. Meet contemporaries
for cocktails until we're mellow.
Afternoon, evening, they've got my back.
Then cab home and hit the sack.

What do they know, those worrisome friends,
raising an eyebrow, offering a critique
of my daily habits, my weekends?
More than three a day, seven a week?
What I put up with! After all,
aren't I upright? Aren't I functional?

When the Dam Broke

Afterward, when the waters withdrew,
she beheld what remained behind—
the buckled floors, the layers of silt,
the basement carpet, nearly new,
drenched belongings dragged outside.

And she felt helpless to decide
what was gone and what too dear—

Mom's ceramic pot, the patchwork quilt,
tax returns bundled and complete,
photos chronicling every year,
penciled recipes she used to serve,
a plaster cast of the baby's feet.

What to pitch, what to preserve
from all that pain piled in the street?
She was flooded with doubt and fear—
punishment she did not deserve.
So much for faith and frequent prayer!

Then strangers arrived to volunteer,
enabling her to persevere.

Flight

for Mitchell Nugent, artist

He was usually the last chosen for games.
Often he did not even turn out for the choosing.
Forced into boxing, he learned to parry,

to dodge. He developed sleight of hand,
magician of his true purposes,
disguised to himself as much as to others.

Always smaller, with no heart or talent
for fielding or evading a ball of any size,
middling student in the standard curriculum,

he grew indoor skills.
Where juggling words and numbers
mattered most, he was a story problem.

Others more defined by sports
sat silent in the presence of his pencil-work,
his play with crayon, chalk, clay, wood, metal.

Nothing I did on a diamond or court
approached his ability to see and to render,
faithful to what was there and what he imagined

might be, should be there. The last time
we met his portfolio included a Pegasus.
He dissected a hawk to get the wings right,

to locate the secret of being airborne. Full of secrets
himself, he struggled to find his own wings,
organic to himself, to lift off.

Drinking Song

Francis Slee
lived on the slough,
which was a risky thing to do.

One night he drank
a hooch or two
of some of his best basement brew.

He fell into the sea and sank.
So raise a glass to Mr. Francis.
Sing a toast to Mr. Slee.

Praise God for all
our second chances
that that was neither you nor me.

Box Score

This is order. The numbers reassure.
The rest of the world may be off the rails,
but baseball's OPS percentage is true and pure,
a revelation that never fails

to settle your mind and barstool dispute.
Sure, the home team wallows in the basement,
the roster assembled with glue and spit,
but that kid's wins-against-replacement

in low-A ball promises a future.
Possibly next year. Maybe this season.
Likewise you value that rule 5 catcher
whose pop time gives us reason

to believe opponents itching to steal
or wander off first may hesitate a bit.
Mathematics knows beyond *feel*,
beyond *I know it when I see it,*

beyond even the best naked eye
who can cover ground and who cannot.
For whatever you wish to identify
there is a formula. There is a stat.

There are new-fangled conjuring tools.
Though some still parlay by the orthodox
written and unwritten rules,
the knowing abracadabra outside the box.

III.

*Love May Be Wiser
      Than Anyone Knows*

Almost Eleven Years

She no longer sat at the kitchen door.

When put out, she mostly slept
under the lilacs, under the step.

No gift of rodent anymore
lay waiting for us in the dawn,
a trophy from her midnight hunt.

A foundling, a long-haired runt
we'd bathed until the fleas were gone.

Now she didn't speak, didn't complain.
She ignored the nuggets in her dish.

We tried beef, a bit of fish.
Both ended in the compost bin
and in a week were gone to dust,

and when she died, as all cats must,
we shoveled through the crust
of ice, and lay her, weightless, in.

Next morning I expected her
to greet me coming down the stairs
or later curled on my chair,

a cloud of gray, electric fur.

Jackie Winter

A small, gray-brown bird
of much charm and great lore
trills before dawn, a melodious word,
enchanting and often heard—
this outback raconteur.

But now in the bush, trees
blacken beneath January's flame.
While dingoes flee the dead dog days,
while wallabies and koalas fry,
she does not sing her name.

All Kitten Behavior is Hunting Behavior

(from *The Tribe of Tiger*, E.M. Thomas)

Having lost the cat beloved for a decade
we visited the shelter, cages stacked high.
In one, a large tabby, beginning to fade,
slumped in a corner, no longer spry

or interested or truly awake.
Such a pet didn't make much sense.
More like a rumpled pillow
lacking wonder and innocence.

We noticed two eight-week kittens,
litter-mate brothers, wobbling
around on black and white mittens.
When lifted they weighed nothing

but presented their faces, forlorn,
pleading. At home, after a day
learning the ropes, they were reborn,
stalking our curtains like jungle prey.

The Halloween Hordes

Satan flapping in the spruce
attracts pirates on the loose.
One sports a patch. One, a sword
to ravage this evening's smorgasbord.

His neck snug in a hangman's noose,
Frankenstein's monster shuffles toward
the lantern at our ancient house,
seeking the wholesome candy store.

Hulk, a chemically altered green,
glows in the dark, a brute—
the most muscular child ever seen.
She requests an apple or citrus fruit.

Now Dracula flutters in cowl and suit,
a gauzy princess, a dinosaur.
A corpse, decay beyond dispute,
displays a claw and oozing sore,

helps himself to the caramel loot.
Like all the others—an omnivore.

Daily Routines

This is the home where Gimpel and Gus,
littermate tuxedos, climb the shelves,
topple a planter, an heirloom vase.

Mornings they arouse a fuss,
amazing their masters if not themselves.
Explaining would be extraneous.

Most un-feline. Spontaneous
in their DNA, they stalk,
stare, crouch, attack.

When the sun is high, they tell us
it's time to sprawl on the walk,
to experience warmth on the back,

the give of grass beneath their paws,
arching at the pine to quicken claws.
Then inside going Rip Van Winkle

on the couch, the afghan. They doze
as if still embryos,
intertwined brothers, Gus and Gimpel,

each other's pillow, harmonic snore.
Earlier they appeared at war,
but those take-downs seem superficial,

less so for an infant mouse or mole
whom they occasionally swallow whole.
God's creatures, mostly civil.

Thanksgiving

for Kacy, Ryan, Michael, Andrew, and Matty Z.

Today of all days think of the full table.

May loved ones gather as they are able
from their otherwise have to's and must do's.

Today may you choose
otherwise, full embraces, full smiles.

Put aside absences, silences, the years,
slights, deeper wounds, the miles.

The chasm between the candles disappears.
Pass the bread, your hand, a single word.

A memory, misplaced, reappears,
a face, a voice. We have prepared

a table before you. Come, take your seat
with us. Here is your wine.

Today may you heal and be clean
and be complete.

Winter Games

We stomped pathways in the mushy snow.
winding around trees, with an occasional box
where the chick found haven from the fox.

Predator and prey—but now and then
when my brother put pedal to the metal,
I lost footing, butt over tea kettle.

I lay there in my woolens, soaked,
dead weight, snared by his stealth,
both of us laughing and out of breath.

Then I was the fox, and so it went,
a Saturday morning, Sunday afternoon,
until spring came, and we moved on

to planting, weeding, mowing the lawn,
grown-up chores, arriving too soon.

Fine

A young man dressed in baggy blue
checks my first and final name,
and underneath, age seventy-two,
a number, which, however true,
is startling all the same.

I'm here for my November draw,
one of two received each year.
A little pick, and then the flow
of life, one that began long ago,
revealing I'm still in the clear.

We hope. On the whole I feel good,
if unable to rise at dawn
and run the effortless way I would
when I was younger of breath and blood,
travelling the road all runners run.

Afterwards, in the hospital lot,
a woman makes her listing way
to the electric door I just came out.
She is stooped, face lined with doubt,
wind ruffling her hair, thin and gray.

I offer her my once strong arm.
Her other clutches a wooden cane.
She says she's bracing for a storm.
Her coat, misbuttoned, in disarray,
billows on this late Fall day.

She wishes me, *Good afternoon.*
Feels obligated to explain
her infirmities, and then,
once in her cart, she says she's fine.
Thanks me once. And then again.

Audition Tips for Children

Even if you are tall for your age,
heftier than your classmates,
do not assume your voice carries
to the far brick wall
where a committee scribbles notes.
Give it to them. Give your all.

Do not assume your normal voice—
breakneck on the playground,
pell-mell at your lockers,
warp speed with lunch buddies—
will work. If your lines sound
like you are chewing Skittles,

consider pausing, slowing down.
If playing, for example, the Goose,
do not assume your gander rocks
like a teenager. Even if God
did not make you bold, let loose.
Make witnesses applaud.

If you are reading for the Mouse,
squeak within range of the human ear.
Remember: Audience! Audience!
If you growl too throaty as the Cat,
you may enjoy it, but will they hear?
Though you may laugh, they may not.

Whatever your role, your purpose is
to weave a story. To entertain.
Grandma has driven a hundred miles
to behold and embrace your Pig.
Don't make the lovely lady strain.
Whatever your part—Be Big.

Season of Mists

This morning we close and lock the windows,
set the thermostat, flip the furnace on.

We remove summer sheets, cover the pillows
with flannel, spread a comforter billowy with down.

Our bushes blaze before losing their leaves.
Our cats stalk stink bugs that want indoors,

hunting less of their nights and daily lives,
more of it dozing on warmer floors.

Darkness, unwelcome, arrives before dinner.
Dawn takes its sweet time re-entering the room.

We grow fat like bears, while days grow thinner;
the basement, the couch, becoming home.

Reluctantly, in layers, we leave our lairs.
We travel less often up and down the stairs.

Dropout

He joined scouts, so I did, too.
He demonstrated proper tilt to his hat,
how to look shipshape in gold and blue.
He insisted I learn the Code by heart,

led me on hikes, boiled hunter stew,
spotted a red-tail hawk and woodland rat.
Looping around and through,
he taught exacting knots like that.

He earned awards, Lion to Bear,
a chestful of badges, his Webelos.
His life centered on campfire,
regiment, creased clothes.

So why did I not feel esprit de corps?
Why did every word seem a compromise
recited by rote, a passionless prayer,
marching orders I never chose?

I did not want to be on anyone's clock,
swim to the closest barrel and back,
chow on cue with the rest of the flock,
or swear by the Law of the Pack.

At the Beach, IMHO

I mean no person any wrong
but not every caboose merits a thong.

Sure, a baby's bottom, plump and nude,
is the cutest thing in pulchritude.

Offensive? Only to a prude.
But at a certain age a keister's cheeky

(except for Gauguin's girls in Tahiti).
For shyer folks, it's not that cool

to display one's bum. At the pool
I keep my drawers on as a rule.

Books in the Dumpster

These speak to no one anymore.
No more mysteries to unravel.
Now they rot, and we are poor--
goodbye Akhmatova. Aristotle farewell.

Goodbye Dickinson. Goodbye Wiesel.
Goodbye *Utopia* and Thomas More.
Champions of civility—Swift, Orwell—
phrases curling in smoke and fire.

Purses empty of their pearls.
Trees silent, and the small birds.
Lost are we. Lost boys and girls
at a loss for words.

The Beer Truck

for Julie Johnston, AAMS

Now and then we raise a glass.
Maybe more now than when we were young.
As we grow, we develop a tongue
for brew with bite, tang, and sass
that helps the aging heart take wing.

When we travel to those years—
of ankles, shoulders, hips, and knees
clicking like castanets, a swarm of bees
buzzing between the ears,
medicine fogging the mind and eyes—

inevitably we turn a page
toward the ever-approaching night.
Or, put more gently, we eat the goat,
then ride across the purple sage
into the far and dimming light.

Eventually, we're shit outta luck.
So, what'll it be? Crossing a road,
burdened by life's unbearable load
when in a blink we're thunderstruck—
blindsided by the barreling truck?

Hey, Jenny—exploding over the street?
Irish mother's milk, a Guinness?
Something bold, unmistakably British?
A Belgian heavy with winter wheat?
Tecate, it's lightly bitter finish?

O Tannenbaum

Listen: There's a lesson here.
One bulb from this time last year
has died. So the entire strand
is dark, lacking yuletide cheer.

Our evergreen's leaning in its stand
Eastward toward the Holy Land.
Not much holding it save prayer
and all sustaining it by hand.

You can almost hear great-grandma swear
Jesus, Mary, and Balthazar.
Eventually, rituals almost right,
we fix atop the tree a star

flickering into the frostbitten night,
however brief, however far.

The Closing of the Frontier

May the Great Spirit smile on your little town...

I thought I was a child for a long time.
I could not imagine not being a child
awakening at dawn with the tame
Comanche horses in the wild.

This was Saturday at dawn.
The den, a great plain, was still,
a canvas I could draw upon,
stacking books upon a hill.

Upstairs my brother was sleeping in.
Even my father was still asleep,
his breath rumbling like an engine,
his day's news asleep on the stoop.

I was Johnny, the half-Kiowa,
leathery brown, a force
for good on my appaloosa.
Like the Holy Man Crazy Horse

I tried to dream myself into the real world
as I did without trying when I was seven.
But no visions or stories called
to me now that I was past eleven

and had no idea where they should go.
I tried to picture brother bear and antelope,
the prairie, the great herds of buffalo.
But both rider and pony seemed asleep.

I returned them all--adversaries, sidekicks,
Quanah Parker, horsemen, the pioneers--
to the empty box, along with the books,
my vast and now vacant frontiers.

Mother's Day, 2018

You would be one hundred.
Decades of cigarettes did you in.
Now you sip wine, are well-fed.
Your hair is neither gray nor thin.

You are not alone. Instead
you and Dad sway to a Goodman tune.
Your hair is long, your shoes red.
It is 1941 and will always be June.

Someone's crying, but after Kaddish
there is life, an under-the-breath
snark in both English and Yiddish.
The parlor rings with belly laugh.

When Helen winks, you wink back.
Your smooth hands smooth the tablecloth.
We tear a lapel, dress all in black.
You are beautiful, even in death.

Overheard at the Donut Shop

Every Sunday they chew the fat
over steaming coffee and gooey treats.

Today they squeeze into corner seats
near where their companion sat.

Was her passing unexpected?
Do God's wonders never cease?

May she sleep in heavenly peace
until her soul be resurrected.

Are things ever what they seem?
Who can fathom His mysterious ways?

They stare out the window, as in a dream,
exhaling slowly. Then one says,

Would you pass the maple glaze?
I know you prefer Bavarian Cream.

Old Friends in the Park

What can I say that I haven't said?
What can you hear that you haven't heard?
Say, toss that dove a crust of bread,
the spotted gray, the one-legged bird.

Quit your stalling and move your pawn.
Why do you bother? You know I'll win.
Did you hear? Antonio's gone.
Saw Mr. Death and said *Come in.*

Grab a cold one. Pull up a chair.
Just like that. Hey, move your knight.
Jeez, you're blind. God, I swear
you can't tell the black queen from the white.

What can I see that I haven't seen?
How many years we been playing this board?
Boy, those pigeons sure are mean.
When you want to leave just say the word.

Blessed Arrangement

The strangest newspaper item yet:
a man keeping an alligator for a pet.

He claimed she alleviated his anxiety
at home, if not in polite society.

He enjoyed the music when she hissed,
was cheaper than a psychiatrist.

But what his condo manager fears
is when a neighbor disappears.

Colleagues, over for a shot and a song,
never linger very long.

I ask *Why not a pup or parakeet?*
One can pounce, the other tweet.

Can't other creatures be of service
addressing your nature to be nervous?

Gossips could not comprehend
such devotion to his reptilian friend,

her shining claws and sighing snout.
An uncommon marriage I do not doubt.

But as they say *One person's meat,*
well-done or rare, is another's mate.

Why should he care what people suppose?
Love may be wiser than anyone knows.

Acknowledgments

Several poems in this collection appeared in the following publications:

The Orchards Poetry Journal
Almost Eleven Years
Packing
Ode to the Melanzana
Come Live With Me and Be My Love

Third Wednesday
Board Meeting
Almost Eleven Years
Season of Mists
That Blessed Arrangement

The New Verse. News
George from Poland

I am grateful to Rob Hyner of Avon, Connecticut (hynerphotoart.com) for the cover image *Apples and Oranges.* A talented photo artist, Rob is also a treasured friend.

Many thanks to poets and editors Kyle McCord and Nick Courtright of Atmosphere Press for their astute and patience guidance. Without question this book is better due to their insights and encouragement.

This book is dedicated to Cheryl, whose *love is wiser than anyone knows.*

About the Author

Larry Levy's poems have appeared in *The Orchards Poetry Journal, Third Wednesday, South Carolina Review, The Virginia Quarterly Review,* and other little and online magazines. In 2019 his poem *Almost Eleven Years* was nominated by the editors of *The Orchards Poetry Journal* for a Pushcart Prize.

His recently published collections are *All the Dead are Holy* (Atmosphere Press, 2016) and *What Outlives Us* (Atmosphere Press, 2017).

An earlier book *I Would Stay Forever If I Could and New Poems* is in a second expanded printing from Mayapple Press. He has also published *Three Things That Have Nothing to Do With Teaching,* a collection of reflective logs.

Retired from teaching at every level from pre-school to graduate school, Larry and his wife Cheryl live in Midland, Michigan where they direct plays and coach others on acting and writing.

www.ingramcontent.com/pod-product-compliance
Lightning Source LLC
Chambersburg PA
CBHW032122050726
47590CB00008B/2929